Great Pyrenees
Pictorial History
Volume III
Color

By

Joseph B. Gentzel

Published by

Pyrenean Journal

an imprint of
Your Pet Place Administration, Inc.
29 Galilee Church Road
Jefferson, GA 30549 USA

First Edition
Copyright 2009
Pyrenean Journal

PJ

No part of this book may be copied or reproduced without the express written permission of Pyrenean Journal

Great Pyrenees
Pictorial History   Volume III- Color

Joseph B. Gentzel and Nicholas June, 2008

Pictured above with me is Champion Talisman Patron les Enfants d'Aneto aka Nicholas. Nicholas is my son, at least to my soul

This is my fifth book on the Great Pyrenees. Three in this Pictorial History series plus **Great Pyrenees Owner's Handbook** published in 2008 and my first book, **The Great Pyrenees-From France With Love** published in 2002. I also wrote a book of fiction using the Great Pyrenees as the central character, **Roi; Shepherd King's Dog** published in 2008. Nicholas was the prototype for "Roi," my Great Pyrenees hero in the book. All are available at Amazon.Com.

My beautiful wife these past 45 years, Maryann and I began our love affair with the majestic Great Pyrenees in 1972. Our involvement and travels related to the study and interest in the breed has led to the wealth of information and pictures contained in these books. After six children (five boys and one girl) we find ourselves immersed in the breed full time. Maryann paints and helps with the kennel. I write and help with the kennel as well. Along the way we have owned and bred over 100 Champions and done about all that we have wanted to do relative the Great Pyrenees. I set up and administer a social network on the web, **Great Pyrenees Community** or **GPC** that has members from all over the world at www.toppooch.ning.com. Join us there, you will have fun and learn every day about our wonderful dogs.

Great Pyrenees
Pictorial History   Volume III- Color

My youngest son, Gaelen Gentzel continues with the breed and devotes his full time to life as a busy professional handler.

Front cover of Roi; Shepherd King's Dog

Painting on the cover is by the great naïve Haitian master painter Wilson Bigaud titled **Manger Scene**, done in 1965. The cameo picture is of Nicholas depicting "Roi." Roi, a Great Pyrenees, is the main character and hero in my book of fiction.

Great Pyrenees
Pictorial History   Volume III- Color

Tour of Great Pyrenees Country

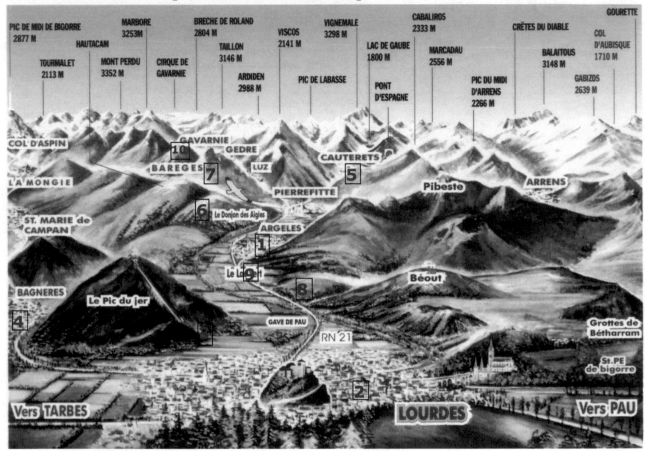

In the above view we are looking south toward Spain.

1. Argelès Gazost was the home of Eugène Byasson who formed the CCP or Argelès Club circa 1907. It is also the present location where the RACP holds its annual specialty show every year.

2. Lourdes was where de Soum, Pic de Jer, and Betpouey had Great Pyrenees kennels. It is also the location of Château Fort seen to the left of the number and the Grotto of Saint Bernadette on the right of the number.

3. Pic de Jer mountain was the location of the kennel of de Soum. Not to be confused with Pic de Jer, the breeder in Lourdes.

4. Bagnères de Bigorre is the location where the citizens in that village made a gift to Field Marshall Viscount Alanbrooke of a Great Pyrenees dog named Bédat de Monda after WWII.

5. Cauterets is the birth place of Bernard Sénac-Lagrange. It was also the place where the Pastour Club held its historic dog show in 1907. Madame

Harper visited and purchased dogs to bring back to England. Some of Mr. and Mrs. Crane's early imports to America came via the famous market in Cauterets. On up the road is Pont d'Espagne and Lac de Gaube on the Spanish border.

6. Benoît Cockenpot has his Pic de Viscos kennel off the road to Hautacam, perched high on the mountain side southeast of Argelès-Gazost.

7. Barèges is the area where the young Dauphine (later Louis VI) found his "Patou" in 1675 and returned with him to the Louvre. In 1677 the Marquis de Louvois found his "Patou" at the village of Betpouey in this same area. The Great Pyrenees became court dog under Louis IV reign.

8. Viger is a small village just south of Lourdes and right off RN21 that was the location of the kennel "Viger." They owned Sultan de Viger, an important "bridge" dog from WWII to the Comte de Foix kennel.

9. Monsieur and Madame Esquerre have their kennel, Val du Levandan, along RN21 just north of Argelès-Gazost at Agos-Vidalos. Look for the sign on right traveling south.

10.   Gavarnie, a beautiful little village high in the mountains at a glacier, has historically been known to have a village "Patou."

No "Patous" seen in Betpouey today, but then again we were not the young Dauphine or the Marquis de Louvois.

Photo Gillianne Gentzel

Betpouey visit 2002-
L-R Joseph B. Gentzel, Maryann Gentzel & Jan Waitz in 2002.

Chasse aux Loups **by Jean Baptiste Oudry circa 18th century**

To me this is the classic depiction of this wonderful breed from antiquity to contemporary times. Most of the pictures of this painting are so dark it's hard to make out the wolf, but this one is quite good although somewhat flawed.

Photo courtesy Jan Geritis

Chasse aux Loups

A Bay Horse and A White Dog

Painted by Georges Stubbs in 1769. From the archives of the International Great Pyrenees Review.

Detail of A Bay Horse and A White Dog

Great Pyrenees
Pictorial History   Volume III- Color

Old Lithograph

We have seen this old lithograph before in black and white, but it is quite striking in its gold tones.

Great Pyrenees
Pictorial History   Volume III- Color

Cabas by Thomas M. Joy- Queen Victoria's Pyrenean Mountain dog circa 1848

Samuel Taylor Middleton by Andrew B. Carlin 1852 [1]

---

[1] See volume one, page 20 for more information on this painting and artist.

Old lithograph "Le Chien des Pyrénées" from the 19th Century

Old lithograph "Bear Hunt" from 19th Century

Great Pyrenees
Pictorial History   Volume III- Color

Post card depicting Saint Bernadette, the patron saint of shepherds

Transhumance

Pâtres Pyrénéens au 19e Siècle

19th Century Lithograph of a Great Pyrenees with people

National Geographic Magazine color plate

A Friendly Gesture-Attributed to Herring,Sr. 1847

Great Pyrenees
Pictorial History   Volume III- Color

Chateau Fort in Lourdes, France

The Chateau Fort in Lourdes, France was a fortified fort in ancient France that employed Great Pyrenees as guardians for the fort. Today it houses the Pyrenean Museum that has a collection of Great Pyrenees items. In the left background is Pic de Jer the scenic mountain site that housed the kennels of de Soum of Monsieur Cazaux-Moutou.

Old colored post card of "Viscos"

Courtesy RACP

Traditional scene

Milanollo Néthou by Maud Earl Circa early 20th Century

Great Pyrenees
Pictorial History   Volume III- Color

Old post card colored

Old post card

Old New Year's greeting post card

Great Pyrenees
Pictorial History   Volume III- Color

Club de Argelès Pups circa early 20th century

Illustrates the grizzled "Blaireau" term applied to most colors in Great Pyrenees.

European Badger

Old 19th century lithograph

Great Pyrenees
Pictorial History   Volume III- Color

Vol.XXV - N°303   1er Septembre 1928

VIE A LA CAMPAGNE

PAOÛ DU GIVRE
GRAND PYRÉNÉEN
VEDETTE DE CINÉMA

HACHETTE   Prix de ce Numéro: 5 Fr.
Apartir du 1er Décembre 1928: 6 Fr.

1928 magazine cover of Vie a la Campagne with Paoü du Givre

21

Hutchinson's Dog Encyclopedia magazine cover 1935

Great Pyrenees pictured on the cover is Estat d'Argeles and Estagel d'Argeles.

Great Pyrenees
Pictorial History   Volume III- Color

Color plate by Nina Scott Langley from 1935 Hutchinson's Dog Encyclopedia

Chevy working 2007

"Chevy" is American & Canadian Champion Aneto Like A Rock who lives with his owners Susan and Brian Price in Canada. Chevy is a multiple AKC and Canadian Working Group placing Great Pyrenees. Bred by Joe and Maryann Gentzel.

Photo Susan Price

Great Pyrenees
Pictorial History   Volume III- Color

Painting by Edward Miner appearing in National Geographic Magazine

Great Pyrenees
Pictorial History   Volume III- Color

Estat d'Argeles & Estagel d'Argeles-painting by S. Edwin Megargee

Post card from Pyrenees Mountains "Les Amis"

Urdos de Soum-painting by S. Edwin Megargee 1937.

Urdos de Soum was the first dog Mr. and Mrs. Crane imported and became the first champion of the breed in America.

Great Pyrenees working with sheep

Great Pyrenees
Pictorial History   Volume III- Color

Mary Crane with unidentified Great Pyrenees on left.

This painting was found in Mrs. Crane's attic in Massachusetts by the new owner years later. Painting by Miss Clara Greenleaf Perry. Ms. Perry was the Aunt to the two sisters Hedge who had those adorable puppies, Bazen de Soum and Nethou de Soum that Mr. and Mrs. Crane saw that first day when they fell in love with the breed. This simple event led to the Cranes lifelong work on behalf of the breed. Ms. Perry was a well-known artist who spent much time in Europe. Ms. Perry located and procured those two Great Pyrenees puppies for the sisters Hedge directly from Monsieur Cazaux-Moutou of de Soum kennels in Lourdes, France.

Great Pyrenees
Pictorial History   Volume III- Color

Post card from the Pyrenees Mountains

Great Pyrenees
Pictorial History   Volume III- Color

Post card from the Pyrenees Mountains

SOUVENIR DES HAUTES PYRÉNÉES

Post card from Pyrenees Mountains

Great Pyrenees
Pictorial History   Volume III- Color

Martin and Hampus in Norway

Martin aka Cubilon's Hann-Hund Hommage is owned by Hilde Stenstad and Hampus aka Cubilon's Kubric Kastellan both bred by Hilde Dalos Aune in Norway.

Hilde Stenstad and Ruben aka Alta Colina's Don Diablo taken Easter 2009

Great Pyrenees
Pictorial History   Volume III- Color

Post card Pyrenees Mountains

National Dog Show at Olomouc, Czech Republic 2009

Post card from Pyrenees Mountains

Post card Pyrenees Mountains

Great Pyrenees
Pictorial History   Volume III- Color

PYRÉNÉES

Pyrenees Mountain post card

Great Pyrenees
Pictorial History   Volume III- Color

Photo courtesy RACP

Transhumance is still practiced in the Pyrenees Mountains

Picture by Jospeh Gentzel in 2004

Great Pyrenees are still seen with the sheep flocks in Pyrenees Mountains

Pontoise Dogs on Cover of _Rustica_ Magazine, November 19, 1950 edition

Monsieur Andre Delattre with some of his dogs whimsically depicted on the cover of _Rustica_ Magazine in France.

Great Pyrenees
Pictorial History   Volume III- Color

Mrs. Crane in England with Pondtail Tatoo

Great Pyrenees Puppy trading card

Great Pyrenees
Pictorial History   Volume III- Color

Ruth Graham, as a child, running to meet her father Billy Graham.

Ruth Graham followed closely by the family Great Pyrenees, Belshazzer. From Ruth Graham's book, <u>A Legacy of Faith</u>[2]. Ruth Graham, in a email to me about the picture and dog, described Belshazzer as "their most beloved family pet." Photo circa mid 1950's.

---

[2] Graham, Ruth : <u>A Legacy of Faith: Things I learned from My Father</u>, 2006, Inspirio, 5300 Patterson Avenue SE, Grand Rapids, MI 49530,

Edith Smith judging May 6, 1979.

Shown with Mrs. Smith is Maryann Gentzel and Aneto Benchmark.

Great Pyrenees
Pictorial History   Volume III- Color

Quibbletown Jim Dandy patch made by Edith K. Smith.

Edith Smith was an art major in college. That talent is showcased in this handmade patch of her favorite dog, Quibbletown Jim Dandy. She did it for a small purse she made and donated to a Great Pyrenees auction circa late 1960's. Jim Dandy won the Great Pyrenees Club of America's National Specialty in 1964 and again in 1966.

Great Pyrenees blending in with its flock

Great Pyrenees
Pictorial History   Volume III- Color

Seaver Smith and Edith Smith with Quibbletown Jim Dandy

Jim Dandy was Edith's favorite. Picture taken at Laneway Farm in 1974.

La Vie Canine magazine-January, 1979

NOTRE COUVERTURE

Chien de montagne des Pyrénées

Ronchon des Crocs Blancs de Tenimerf
née le 13 juin 1968, à M. Freminet, 16,
rue A.-de-Musset, 94 - St-Maur (Tél. :
383-26-11), par Oural de la Franche Pierre
appartenant à Mme Dingremont, et
Kaline du Manoir de Ricquemesnil.

Great Pyrenees
Pictorial History   Volume III- Color

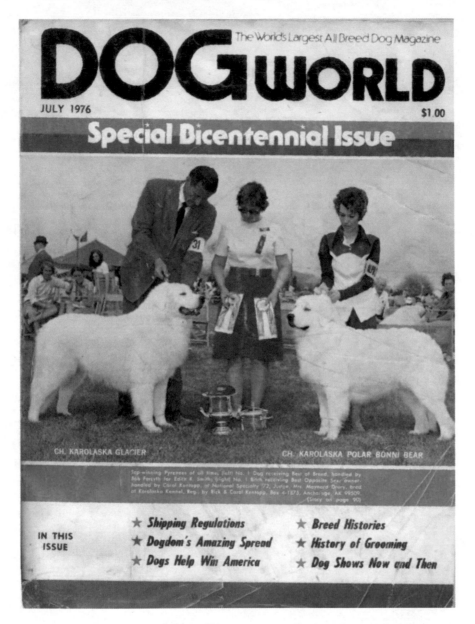

July 1976 Bicentennial Issue of Dog World Magazine

On the cover were littermates Karolaska Glacier and Karolaska Polar Bonni Bear winning Best of Breed and Best of the Opposite Sex at the GPCA National Specialty show. Glacier on left is handled by Robert Forsyth and Bonnie is handled by Carol Kentopp, their breeder. The judge is Mrs. Maynard Drury. Dog World Magazine at the time was the "standard" magazine for the pure bred dog world in North America. Glacier was owned by Seaver and Edith Smith of Quibbletown.

Soleil Pierre de Blu Crest was Best of Breed at the 1974 GPCA National Speciality

Pierre is shown above with the judge on left, Mrs. Joan Passini-Birkett, his owner/handler Vic Capone and his breeder Jack Magoffin.

Great Pyrenees
Pictorial History   Volume III- Color

Great Pyrenees post card from France

Great Pyrenees
Pictorial History   Volume III- Color

Monaco stamp 1977

Playing card "10 of diamonds"

Great Pyrenees
Pictorial History   Volume III- Color

Mary Crane the judge, awards a Working Group One win to Karolaska Glacier circa 1970's

Glacier is shown by his owner Seaver Smith. Mrs. Crane also awarded a Working Group One win to Karolaska Captivator aka "Harvey" owned by Joseph and Maryann Gentzel. Harvey went on that day to win Best In Show.

Basque of Basquaerie gravestone in the Monroe Cemetery, Duxbury, VT.

Great Pyrenees
Pictorial History   Volume III- Color

Bagnères de Bigorre - 18-4-82

Street scene at Bagnères de Bigorre, France 1982

Leah and Cameron about 2003.

Osteosarcoma (bone cancer) is a scourge on the breed. In this photo Leah, on left, had a recent amputation for osteosarcoma.

A MON MAÎTRE

Puisque nos vies se sont croisées, toi mon maître
Fais que nous restions toujours de vrais amis.
Comme je te donne ma fidélité, garde moi la tienne
A moi qui n'hésite pas à voler à ton secours,
Donne ta protection sans compter !
Donne moi des ordres clairs et j'obéirai,
Ne me bat jamais si je n'ai pas compris !
Pour une caresse, je te suivrai partout...
Car une promenade avec toi fais mon bonheur !
Et surtout ne m'abandonne jamais
Car, moi, je ne le ferai pas.

Post card from the Pyrenees Mountains

Great Pyrenees
Pictorial History   Volume III- Color

Duché de Savoy kennle graphic

This septa like graphic was used by Duché de Savoy to depict their kennel in the 1990's. Monsieur Raymond Ducrey was one of the successful breeders during this period of time in France.

Photo Joseph Gentzel

Bletterans in 1987

The open bitch class at Bletterans, France in 1987 for the French National Specialty show. The judge, standing on right, is Dr. Vigouroux.

Great Pyrenees engaging Bears in Norway.

Estom du Comte de Foix was Best of Breed at the 1992 French National Specialty

Great Pyrenees
Pictorial History   Volume III- Color

Great Pyrenees bitch--Pyrenees Mountain winter scene post card.

Old Great Pyrenees trading card

Telling the Tale, **signed print by artist Mike Atkinson from Great Britain**

Post card from Pyrenees Mountains

La Prière
du Chien des Pyrénées

Tout petit, boule de neige,
je fais la joie des enfants.
Adulte, ma masse imposante
n'a rien de rassurant.
Pourtant, ma vocation est bien
pacifique, je suis les traces sur
les pistes, je flaire, je cherche,
je retrouve l'égaré, et toute
angoisse est dissipée.
Tu es fier de moi, O mon
maître, ton regard me le dit.
Je te donne la patte,
nous nous sommes compris

Post card from the Pyrenees Mountains-"La Pière du Chien des Pyréneés"

Post card from the Pyrenees Mountains

Great Pyrenees
Pictorial History   Volume III- Color

Post card from the Pyrenees Mountains

Great Pyrenees
Pictorial History   Volume III- Color

Izaux de la Vallée du Girou

Izaux de la Vallée du Girou was Best of Breed at the 1998 French (RACP)
National Specialty show. Owned and bred by Madame Evelyne Galiana.

Great Pyrenees
Pictorial History   Volume III- Color

Pretty in Pink

AKC Champion Ourse du Pic de Viscos bred by Monsieur Benoît Cockenpot in France. Owned by Joseph and Maryann Gentzel.

Great Pyrenees blend in with the flock

Great Pyrenees
Pictorial History   Volume III- Color

Post card from Pyrenees Mountains

Great Pyrenees
Pictorial History   Volume III- Color

Puppies are a popular subject of post cards in the Pyrenees Mountains

Puppies are used in almost any setting for Pyrenees Mountain post cards.

Great Pyrenees
Pictorial History   Volume III- Color

Post card Pyrenees Mountains

Many areas use Great Pyrenees on post cards

Great Pyrenees
Pictorial History   Volume III- Color

Pyrenees Mountains post card

Pyrenees Mountains post card

Great Pyrenees
Pictorial History   Volume III- Color

Post card from Pyrenees Mountains

Pyrenees Mountains post card

Figure 1-Historical reenactment

It's interesting to see historical reenactment scenes in the Pyrenees Mountain region that use Great Pyrenees, often as part of the costume and daily life reenactment. I think it shows how the breed has become engrained in the culture of the region.

Great Pyrenees
Pictorial History   Volume III- Color

Figure 2-Historical reenactment

Figure 3-Historical reenactment

Great Pyrenees
Pictorial History   Volume III- Color

Figure 4-Historical reenactment

Figure 5-Historical reenactment

Great Pyrenees
Pictorial History   Volume III- Color

Figure 6-Historical reenactment scene

Great Pyrenees
Pictorial History   Volume III- Color

Figure 7-Historical reenactment

Figure 8-Historical reenactment

Figure 9- Historical reenactment

Figure 10-Historical reenactment

Post card from Pyrenees Mountains

Post card from Pyrenees Mountains

Great Pyrenees
Pictorial History   Volume III- Color

Post card from Pyrenees Mountains

Pyrenees post card

Great Pyrenees
Pictorial History   Volume III- Color

Photo courtesy Bernadette Ducker

10 week male puppy

Male puppy above is by Champion Honors Bound for Glory, out of Champion Tip'N Chip Mustang Sally, bred by Bernadette Ducker and Karen Bruneau in California. Photo taken April 2009.

Old English cards

Great Pyrenees
Pictorial History   Volume III- Color

Post card Pyrenees Mountains

Post card Pyrenees Mountains

Post card Pyrenees Mountains

Post card Pyrenees Mountains

Post card Pyrenees Mountains

Great Pyrenees
Pictorial History   Volume III- Color

PRIERE DU CHIEN DES PYRENEES

Tout petit, boule de neige, je fais la joie des enfants.
Adulte, ma masse imposante n'a rien de rassurant.
Pourtant, ma vocation est bien pacifique,
je suis les traces sur les pistes, je flaire,
je cherche, je retrouve l'égaré, et toute angoisse est dissipée.
Tu es fier de moi, O mon Maître, ton regard me le dit.
Je te donne la patte, nous nous sommes compris.

Post card Pyrenees Mountains

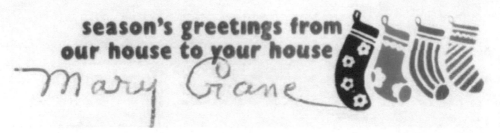

Mrs. Mary W. A. Crane with her dogs on Christmas card

This was used on the cover of Volume II.

Great Pyrenees
Pictorial History   Volume III- Color

Post card from Pyrenees Mountains

Same puppies, in a different setting.

Post card Pyrenees Mountains

Post card Pyrenees Mountains

Post card Pyrenees Mountains

Notice the Estive (shepherd's hut) in the background on the right.

Great Pyrenees
Pictorial History   Volume III- Color

Post card Pyrenees Mountains

Post card Pyrenees Mountains

Post card Pyrenees Mountains

Guardenia Earthshaker aka Erwin

First time I saw Erwin I put him up for Best In Sweepstakes at the 1999 Pyrenean Fanciers of the Northeast (PFNE) Regional Specialty show when he was just six months old. Erwin was bred and owned by Donna Coffman and Carolyn Coffman Moore. He is pictured above with Donna's daughter, Carolyn Moore.

Guardenia Earthshaker

Great Pyrenees
Pictorial History   Volume III- Color

Mrs Mary Crane judging May 7, 1978

What a nasty day for a dog show! Pictured left to right is Karolaska Black Eyed Susan Best of the Opposite Sex, with Joseph B. Gentzel and Peter Baynes,always dapper Englishman who took the wet weather with typical English aplomb, is the professional handler holding Karolaska Captivator (Harvey), Best of
Breed. Harvey and Susie were littermates. Peter Baynes is now a very popular judge.

The weather did not matter though as Harvey went on to win Best in Show that day at the Kennesaw Kennel Club all breed show.

Color drawing of two Great Pyrenees

Dr. Robert M. Brown judging a Great Pyrenees regional specialty 1981.

Pictured with Dr. Brown above is Douglas Holloway, professional handler and Aneto Empress Alexandra,winners bitch at the specialty. The specialty was part of the classes at the Rock Creek Kennel Club in Maryland. Dr. Brown is one of the top Great Pyrenees judges in the world. He has judged many specialties and shows all over the USA and around the world. He is slated to judge the National Specialty of the Great Pyrenees Club of America being held in Lancaster, PA. in 2010. Doug Holloway is now a popular judge.

Great Pyrenees
Pictorial History   Volume III- Color

Great Pyrenees working?

At first glance this appears to be a Great Pyrenees working. Notice the large dun colored dog with the black mask on the left. This could be a Kangal Dog from Turkey. If so, the likelihood of the white dog being a Great Pyrenees is lessened considerably, as the Akbash Dog would be more probable. The Akbash Dog is a very strong candidate to be a direct and very relevant ancestor to the Great Pyrenees. Turkey (Anatolian plateau) is along the migratory trail when nomadic man moved from Asia Minor, westward with his domestic sheep and goats.

Post card from the Pyrenees Mountains

Great Pyrenees
Pictorial History   Volume III- Color

Coming Home **by Arlene Oraby 1995**

"Coming Home" A painting and Poem by Arlene Oraby

Along the way home
on the road's shoulders,
sheep sashay in tune
to a shepherd's steps,
Pyrenees gait in beat,
trees sway inward,
hugging the passage.

A painting—
Of last light, falling,
Caught by hands
in oils of colored rhythm;
for a moment,
time stands still.

Arlene Oraby from New York is one of the top contemporary artists in the world as well as a Great Pyrenees breeder and lover.

She has painted many masterpieces like the one above. This one speaks to us of the intrinsic essence of the ages old rituals between the flock, the shepherd and the Great Pyrenees that protect them all.

The Great Pyrenees **Bronze Statue by Jeff Zinggeler**

This bronze statue of the Great Pyrenees used as its model a Quibbletown style dog. That means a balanced dog with compact features that would undoubtedly move with reach and drive as it worked the flocks day and night. The strength and power is there in combination with the elegance most breeders cherish.

Seaver Smith saw the statue when it was auctioned at the 1997 Great Pyrenees Club of America's National Specialty where he was the judge. His comments were that the bronze statue was a stunning piece of art and a most accurate presentation of the breed.

Great Pyrenees
Pictorial History   Volume III- Color

Photo Courtesy Dale Dougherty

Tip'N Chip Mustang Sally on left & Whitehope Pneuma 2008.

Tip'N Chip Mustang Sally with Gaelen Gentzel, handler, and Alain Pécoult, judge in 2006

Great Pyrenees
Pictorial History   Volume III- Color

Israeli Magazine cover

Great Pyrenees appear in publications all over the world as illustrated by this Israeli magazine cover.

Judy Cooper with Tip'N Chip Foolish Pleasure

Judy and Pleasure on the cover of Canine Chronicle Magazine. Pleasure was one of many top Great Pyrenees bred and owned by Judy Cooper at Tip'N Chip. Tip'N Chip's breeding excellence continues today as it has the past 60 plus years.

Great Pyrenees
Pictorial History   Volume III- Color

Hartza was Best of Breed at the 1996 French National Specialty Show. You can see in 2001 at nine years old she is still quite a beautiful bitch.

Hartza II du Pic de Viscos at 2001 French National Specialty Show

Dieudonne Impyrial Acclaim aka "Fame".

Fame made breed history in 2005 by becoming the first Great Pyrenees to win the Working Group at the prestigious Westminster Kennel Club show at Madison Square Garden in New York City. Pictured above with Fame is his owner/handler, Karen Bruneau. The Group Judge, on the left, is Mr. Norman Kenney.

Great Pyrenees
Pictorial History   Volume III- Color

Aneto Patou 1996

The story of Patou has been on the internet for over 10 years. It's a journal entry account of a working dog. It has been translated into several languages around the world for reprinting there. You can read it in English at http://josephbgentzel.com/patous.htm

Aneto Patou and his "Goose Patrol" at work 1997

Great Pyrenees
Pictorial History   Volume III- Color

Post card Pyrenees Mountains

Post card from the Pyrenees Mountains

Pierre was nearly 10 years old when this picture was taken. The next year he won the National Specialty at ten.

Photo Maryann Gentzel

Soliel Pierre de Blu Crest with owner Vic Capone at home August, 1973.

Quibbletown Val's Heritage aka "Dennis"

Dennis owned by Lois McIntosh in Canada was a top Quibbletown dog in his day and the foundation of a top breeding kennel, Limberlost, in Canada.

Great Pyrenees
Pictorial History   Volume III- Color

The Announcement **by Marie Sagon 2008**

Great Pyrenees
Pictorial History   Volume III- Color

Eastern Star **by Bridget Olerenshaw circa 1970's**

Great Pyrenees
Pictorial History   Volume III- Color

Nothing is cuter than a group of Great Pyrenees Puppies

Photo Joseph Gentzel

Great Pyrenees working in the Pyrenees Mountains with its Shepherd 2004

Note the traditional black Basque beret on the shepherd.

Basque shepherds shearing sheep-"Patou" is never far away.

CHIOTS DES PYRÉNÉES

Great Pyrenees puppies

Great Pyrenees
Pictorial History   Volume III- Color

Currey Photo

Gaelen Gentzel showing a top winning, Best In Show Great Pyrenees 2007

Professional handlers, at the top of their game, like Gaelen Gentzel show their clients dogs at over a hundred dog shows a year. The show dog sport is very popular around the world. Top handlers forge a special bond between their dogs and themselves. The combination between a top dog and a top handler is artistry at its best.

Great Pyrenees
Pictorial History   Volume III- Color

Post card featuring puppies from Pic de Viscos in France.

Post card- More Pic de Viscos puppies

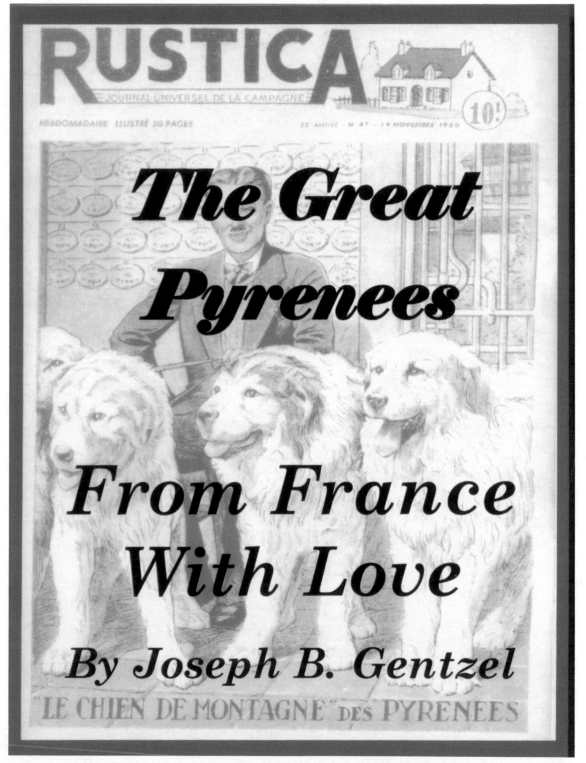

The Great Pyrenees; From France With Love **cover by Joseph B. Gentzel 2002**

Champion Ciel Edith's Legacy d'Aneto AKA "Charlie"

Charlie is a prototype of the style dog that Edith Smith bred at Quibbletown. His Sire, Quibbletown Double Time, was the last Quibbletown stud dog and one of Seaver Smith's favorites.

Post card from the Pyrenees Mountains

Great Pyrenees
Pictorial History   Volume III- Color

Joann Teems judging in 2002.

JoAnn Teems judging the Champions class at the 2002 Great Pyrenees Club of American's National Specialty. Shown is Aneto Etienne with his owner/breeder, Maryann Gentzel.

Valentine's Greeting 2009

The above Valentines greeting was done by graphic artist Melissa Metzler for the Great Pyrenees Community in 2009.

Great Pyrenees
Pictorial History   Volume III- Color

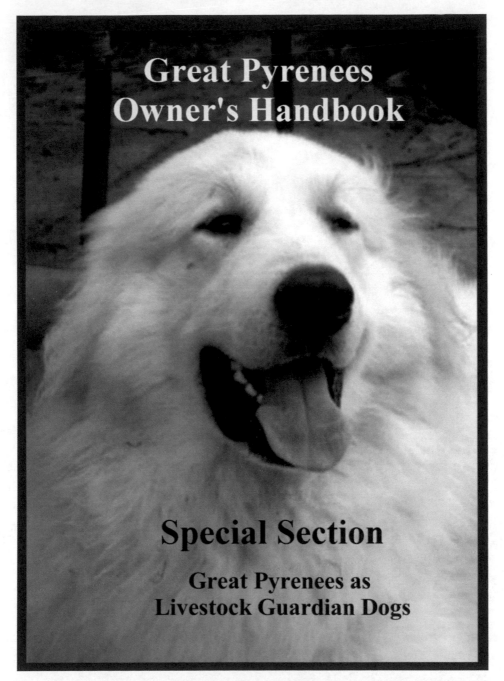

Great Pyrenees Owner's Handbook by Joseph B. Gentzel 2008

Great Pyrenees Owner's Handbook was done to address entry level owner interests, new puppy buyer needs, and those who wanted some basic working information on the breed. The lovely young dog on the cover is "Leo", a son of "Fame." Leo was bred by Joe and Maryann Gentzel at Aneto Great Pyrenees.

Great Pyrenees
Pictorial History   Volume III- Color

"Bliss"- painting by Maryann Gentzel November 21, 2008

Bliss is on the cover of Volume I

Great Pyrenees Community Easter graphic by Melissa Metzler 2009

Great Pyrenees
Pictorial History   Volume III- Color

Murphy, a Great Pyrenees dwarf 2009

One of the genetic problems that has occurred in the United States is the dwarf Great Pyrenees. Presently there is an ongoing study to identify a genetic marker so that breeders can avoid this problem in the future. We are told this project is going very well and every indication is we may soon have that capability.

The dwarf is a very controversial subject filled with extreme emotion on all sides of the issue. The dog above, Murphy, comes from a litter of nine puppies that had four Dwarfs in the litter. Some of the dogs, including Murphy, in the litter work.

It is reported that other genetic problems are associated with the condition. Some dwarfs appear to be otherwise normal (aside from the short statue). Some dwarfs are normal appearing and need diagnosing by a professional with knowledge and experience with this condition. It is done with radiographs.

All responsible breeders agree this genetic problem needs to be eradicated. The dogs we presently have and will continue to have, from time to time, are special little dogs that we all love and feel a strong sense of responsibility for their welfare. Murphy, above, is with Debi and Randy Carpadus in California.

Peggy Watson in Arizona has worked hard on this project for years. The Dwarf Marker project is one supported by the Great Pyrenees Club of America (GPCA). Anyone who believes they have a dwarf should contact Peggy through the GPCA and join the effort to help eradicate this genetic problem.

French post card

Post card from the Pyrenees Mountains

Great Pyrenees
Pictorial History   Volume III- Color

Ça va mon grand?..

Post card from the Pyrenees Mountains

"Thanks for the ride Santa! Wonder when they get up around here?"

Great Pyrenees
Pictorial History   Volume III- Color

Post card from the Pyrenees Mountains

Post card from Pyrenees Mountains

Great Pyrenees
Pictorial History   Volume III- Color

Post card from Pyrenees Mountains

Great Pyrenees
Pictorial History   Volume III- Color

Post card from Pyrenees Mountains

Post card from the famous Col de Tourmalet in Pyrenees Mountains

Great Pyrenees
Pictorial History   Volume III- Color

Post card from Pyrenees Mountains

Post card from Foix in the Pyrenees Mountains

Post card Pyrenees Mountains

Post card Pyrenees Mountains

Aneto Under Grace with handler Gaelen Gentzel. Judge is Dorothy Collier 2008.

Great Pyrenees
Pictorial History   Volume III- Color

Gabriella Mia La Joie Blanche & Lumienkelin Amatsoni in Estonia the winter of 2008.

The two Great Pyrenees above are owned by Marion Silvia Diener in Estonia.

Great Pyrenees
Pictorial History   Volume III- Color

Great Pyrenees and children go hand and hand.

Takita, bred by Pat Ramapuram of Patorama Great Pyrenees from Maryland USA, appears to be reading to his owners grandson. Many of our children have been nurtured by Great Pyrenees.

Ursas Tambel du Bousquetat 7 years of age

Tambel was bred by Phil & Arlene Oraby from New York, USA. He is owned by Ursula Hock-Henschke in the Netherlands.

Great Pyrenees
Pictorial History   Volume III- Color

Framboise Sunpatches Little Lady aka "Patches" owned by Christine Härtel aka "Tina" from Hamburg, Germany.

Patches is a German, Polish, Austrian, and International Champion. Patches was bred by Peggy Watson from Arizona, USA. Tina tells a lovely story on her web site. Having lost their one Great Pyrenees, they (Tina, and her husband Bernd) were lonesome for the Great Pyrenees again in their family. Following are Tina's words:

"No dogs, no walks -the House felt sad and empty. We had to have a new dog - not just any dog -no , it had to be a Pyr . This breed is fascinating. I love the Pyrenean Mountain Dogs- a breed that has retained its self confidence, stubborn ways and endless loyalty to its owners."

Beautiful words, Tina. Patches is striking. We are so glad she came all the way from Arizona to live with you and Bernd in Hamburg.

Great Pyrenees
Pictorial History　　Volume III- Color

Galliagh Navarrah and Syretta Davis

Navarrah was bred by Jenny Haslet from Ireland. Syretta is Jenny's daughter. The love and bond between the two is very apparent.

D'ESPRIT SHANAY LA JOIE BLANCHE bred and owned by Karin Scholten-Elfferich from Holland.

Snow Flake aka "Morris" owned by Hilde Stenstad in Norway

This beautiful red color grizzled with dark gray (grey) is named Arrouye . The color is rare in the breed. It is different than some other reds seen and called "red heads". All the colors are blaireau technically, but this one seems to have the grizzled gray badger mixed with the darker red. Body spots are seen as well. Morris is bred by Kristin Skaare.

Hamish, sitting in front, with his niece Grace and Bruce

Despreaux Highlander aka "Hamish" with Bruce Atkinson and Despreaux Amazing Grace aka "Grace" in Australia. Both dogs owned by Tracy Bassett.

Great Pyrenees
Pictorial History   Volume III- Color

One day old pups

International litter out of Patorama People Whisperer aka "Lily" in Maryland, USA, by Vi'skaly Spirit of Alaska "Spirit" from Sweden. Lily is owned by Olesya and Daniel Grant and was bred by Pat Ramapuram in Baltimore, MD. Spirit is owned and bred by Ingela, Bo and Pernilla Sandström from Sweden.

From a 2009 litter of eleven pups bred and owned by Aurelia Lecomte in France

Neou du Néouvielle

As Madame Arielle Durigneux said, "The great Neou died last November (2008)".

Neou was an incredible dog from a remarkable litter of pups bred in France by Mademoiselle Nadine Lafitte out of a bitch bred by Madame Durigneux in Belgium. His litter brothers were the incredible Noustamic and the beautiful regal Nousty. The three brothers (littermates) dominated the French and surrounding countries show scene for about 10 years.

Neou captured my wounded heart in 2002 at the RACP National Specialty show held at Argelès-Gazost. I have loved him dearly since that day. He was also the toughest dog I think I ever knew. His beauty was exceeded only by his overbearing friendliness for people. Noustamic and Neou were used extensively at stud and Neou came to Canada for awhile and stood at stud In 2006.

Alta Colina's Idar Isbre aka "Izum" was Best of Breed in Russia at 7 months.

Izum was bred by Beate & Berit Konstad in Norway. He is pictured with and owned by Elinasabrina Platonova.

Great Pyrenees
Pictorial History   Volume III- Color

Livestock Guardian Dog puppies. Owned by Deborah Hilliard in New York.

Who says Pyrs are not good in obedience? Smoke, on left, is the first Pyr to gain his Championship, UD title, RAE, and the GPCA Drafting titles. Smoke is the only Pyr to get all the titles. The BDD is for brace draft dog, the only one ever entered to date in this level competition.

Smoke is bred by Patrick Lundberg, Catherine Lundberg and Christine M. Hodel. He is owned by Tommy and Charlotte Bascom.
sire: CH Tip'N Chip Prevailing Wins :
dam: CH Mistral's Maiden Voyage

Way to go Charlotte and Smoke!!

Charlotte Bascom owner of CH Mistral's Doing Things My Way CCG.RAE,UD,(GPCA)-DD,DDX,BDD,VX; aka "Smoke"

Smoke in drafting competition

Great Pyrenees
Pictorial History   Volume III- Color

Index to Captions

Great Pyrenees
Pictorial History   Volume III- Color

Great Pyrenees
Pictorial History   Volume III- Color

Great Pyrenees
Pictorial History   Volume III- Color

Great Pyrenees
Pictorial History   Volume III- Color

Index of People and Dogs

Great Pyrenees
Pictorial History   Volume III- Color

Front Cover

Center picture is Neou du Néouvielle aka Neou. Clockwise from top is Fago de Alba de los Danzante aka "Fago", Guardenia's Earthshaker aka"Erwin", Snow Flake aka "Morris", Dieudonne Impyrial Acclaim aka "Fame", Aneto Leonardo de Puppius Maximus aka "Leo", and Vi'skaly's Spirit of Alaska aka "Spirit".

Neou, bred by Mademoiselle Laffitte, France was owned by Madam Durigneux,Belgium

Fago was bred by Lorenzo Irigoyen Garcés & Nieves Claver Lanaspa, Spain and owned by Tuulikki Tammiala-Salonen, Tuulia Salonen & Juulia Salonen, Finland.

Erwin was bred and owned by Donna Coffman and Carolyn Moore, USA.

Morris is owned by Hilde Stenstad, Norway and bred by Kristin Skaare, Finland.

Fame was bred by Karen Justin, USA and owned by Paul and Karen Bruneau, USA at the time of the photo.

Leo was bred by Joseph and Maryann Gentzel, USA.

Spirit was bred and owned by Ingela, Bo and Pernilla Sandström, Sweden.

Back Cover

"Mudge" owned by Cari Buckman in San Diego, CA, USA was bred by Joseph and Maryann Gentzel, Jefferson, GA USA.

Bottom left- Talisman Patron les Enfants d'Aneto aka "Nicholas" owned by Joseph and Maryann Gentzel, Jefferson, GA USA.

52519558R10075

Made in the USA
Charleston, SC
16 February 2016